G7103

SCHULT

10/03

All I know is that with the approach of summer there comes an increasing yearning to set eyes upon far-off places at the end of the open road. This call when answered is usually termed, "a much needed vacation."

—ELON JESSUP, *THE MOTOR-CAMPING BOOK*, 1921

NEW COVERED WAGON

Across the far horizons of the west
The covered wagon rides the trail again.
No oxen pull it now. This wagon keeps
The swifter, smoother pace of modern men.

From coast to coast it rolls; not months, but days
Now clock the westward course from sea to sea.
The methods change, their purpose is the same,
And turning wheels can still make history.

To go—to see the mountains and the plains;
To leave the noise of cities far behind;
To seek a fairer fate; at least, to flee
The dull monotony of daily grind—

Time has not dulled that urge. The wanderlust
Lives on forever in the hearts of men.
Trails have grown smooth and comfort goes along
As covered wagons travel west again.

—GENE LINDBERG

EVOLUTION

... And then he found the gypsy,
Asleep through all the years,
Awakened in his own staid self,
The nomad call he hears.
The trailer is the answer,
A home behind his car.
In every man the longing
To travel fast and far.
No longer pride of empire,
No wish for house and land.
There's every living comfort
When he joins the trailer band.
He comes and goes at pleasure,
Without roots to hold him fast.
After twenty restless centuries,
Man's freedom comes at last.

—EDITH C. GREGWARE, FROM *TRAILER CARAVAN,* 1937

TRAILER TRAVEL

A VISUAL HISTORY OF MOBILE AMERICA

by Bryan Burkhart • Phil Noyes • Allison Arieff

Gibbs Smith, Publisher
Salt Lake City

FIRST EDITION

06 05 04 03 02   5 4 3 2 1

PUBLISHED BY

Gibbs Smith, Publisher

P.O. Box 667

Layton, Utah 84041

Orders: (800) 748-5439

www.gibbs-smith.com

PREFACE by Phil Noyes

TEXT by Allison Arieff

DESIGN by Bryan Burkhart / MODERNHOUSE

Front matter images:

COVER Illustration from *Home Craft* magazine.

PAGE 1 Red Kelsey advertisement. Courtesy of Vintage Vacations.

PAGE 2 The road ahead. This 1934 Airstream was built by hand from plans bought from Wally Byam. Photograph taken September 1935 near New Laguna, New Mexico. Courtesy of Joyce Fraijo.

PAGE 3 Trailer caravan in the foothills of North Dakota. Photo courtesy of the American Automobile Association Archive.

PAGE 5–6 Trailers on the highway. Courtesy Delmar Watson.

PAGE 7–8 Spartan factory. Courtesy of Vintage Vacations.

PAGE 11–12 Girl at the trailer show. Courtesy Delmar Watson.

PRINTED AND BOUND IN HONG KONG

LIBRARY OF CONGRESS CATALOGING-IN-PUBLICATION DATA

Burkhart, Bryan, 1963–

   Trailer travel : a visual history of mobile America / Bryan Burkhart, Phil Noyes, Allison Arieff.— 1st ed.

    p. cm.

Includes bibliographical references.

  ISBN 1-58685-157-8

  1. Recreational vehicle living—United States History. I. Noyes, Phil. II. Arieff, Allison. III. Title.

  TX1110.B87 2002

  796.7'9—dc21

          2002001678

Here's your cottage by the sea . . .
your cabin by a lake or stream . . .
a lodge in the mountains . . .
a lovely home wherever you are,
all wrapped up in one gleaming aluminum package.

—FROM A SPARTAN TRAVEL TRAILER ADVERTISEMENT, 1946

MOTOR CAMPING
WITH A TENT OR A TRAILER IN TOW
20

SELLING THE DREAM
ADVERTISEMENTS AND PERIODICALS
38

WISH YOU WERE HERE
DISPATCHES FROM THE ROAD
60

TRAILER SHOWS
KEEPING AN EYE ON THE NEW CURVES
70

TAKE A LOOK INSIDE
HEY, THIS IS REALLY NICE . . .
96

I'VE GOT THIS IDEA
DEVELOPMENTS ALONG THE WAY
110

TRAILER LOGOS
CREATING A MEMORABLE IMPRESSION
132

TEARDROPS
KEEPING IT COMPACT
144

WE WOULD LIKE TO THANK

AMERICAN AUTOMOBILE ASSOCIATION OF AMERICA

USC SPECIAL COLLECTIONS

JOHN AGNEW

STEVEN BUTCHER

CRAIG DORSEY

HUELL HOWSER

VINCE MARTINICO

HARRY PALLENBERG

DACE TAUBE

DELMAR WATSON

GEORGE WILKERSON

DAVID WOODWORTH

MORGAN YATES

MARY YEKO

NICK AND JIM

OUR COLLECTIVE MOMS AND DADS

50 Travel Trailers Start Seattle Trek

Decorated with blue and yellow banners, the Los Angeles to Seattle Seafair Caravan of 50 travel trailers departed northward from the Hollywood Bowl parking lot yesterday, after an official sendoff from Lt. Gov. Harold J. Powers.

Sandra Teslow, Queen of the Seattle Seafair, annual aquatic carnival which is the destination of the caravan, received an official message of greeting from Lt. Gov. Powers, in behalf of Gov. Goodwin Knight, which she will deliver to Gov. Albert Rosellini of Washington.

City Councilman Earle D. Baker presented a similar message from Mayor Norris Poulson to Mayor Gordon S. Clinton of Seattle.

Two "horseless carriages" of pre World War I vintage escorted the caravan to the city limits.

James Brunskill, president of the Trailer Coach Association, which sponsors the northward trek, led the caravan on its trip out of the city, followed by the Queen of the Caravan, Mrs. Hildegard Schwarz of Gardena.

The caravaners, all members of travel trailer clubs, will make overnight stopovers at Lake Atascadero, Golden Gate Park, Lake Redding Park, Roseburg and Holiday Park, near the Portland-Vancouver area.

The caravan is slated to arrive at Fort Lawton, Seattle, next Tuesday.

1958 Image and article courtesy of USC Special Collections.

PREFACE

I'd been working on a PBS series called *California's Gold* for about ten years, and I kept hearing about a guy named David Woodworth, who had a huge collection of pre–World War II camping trailers and house cars. For me, a travel trailer was nothing more than an annoyance that I would get stuck behind on two-lane roads, but I decided to take the two-hour drive to see David and his collection. What I saw when I arrived was nothing short of amazing. I had no idea of the important role trailers and house cars have had in our nation's history. David gave me a quick education and a 1936 newsreel that stated there were 250,000 people towing trailers that year. I left knowing that I needed to document this little-known bit of Americana.

I went home and immediately started making calls and doing research. What I found was a wonderful subculture filled with great people who have known about these gems for many years. I met John Agnew and Steven Butcher at Funky Junk Farms, collectors extraordinaire with dozens of vintage trailers between them and a love for all things old. I met Craig Dorsey, who runs Vintage Vacations, a trailer-restoration shop in Anaheim, California, where he turns rusting hulks into magnificent pieces of art. I met Vince Martinico, who has filled two chicken coops with one of the finest collections of trailers and house cars on the planet. And George Wilkerson, proprietor of the Teardrop Fix-It Shop, a man who has done so much to bring these little trailers back into the mainstream. I could go on and on. I once asked John Agnew what his favorite trailer was and he said, "The next one I find." That sort of sums up the obsession that we all share. Every trailer and every scrap of ephemera that we find is a gift.

So after meeting all these people, I knew I had to put together a documentary on the subject, and, much to my wife's chagrin, I became obsessed. Not three weeks from my first meeting with David, I dragged home a 1957 Corvette travel trailer and began to restore it. Several restorations and many trailers later, my wife has actually embraced my insanity and even enjoys helping decorate our trailers. My kids always have an oversized dollhouse to play with, and our visiting guests always look forward to a stay in our unique "guest house." During my research for the documentary, I ended up with so many great images that a book seemed like a natural. And Bryan Burkhart and Allison Arieff (who I met at a Vintage Vacations trailer rally in Felton, California, back in 1999), who'd done such a great job with the book, *Airstream: The History of the Land Yacht,* were the perfect collaborators. With the help of all our trailer friends who have generously allowed us to use their archives, I think we have put together a fun look at this wonderful patch of our nation's colorful quilt.

Phil Noyes

Time and space are at your beck and call, your freedom is complete, and the expense need hardly be more than living at home.

—ELON JESSUP, *THE MOTOR-CAMPING BOOK,* 1921

MOTOR CAMPING

WITH A TENT OR A TRAILER IN TOW

Motor camping emerged not long after the automobile was introduced. This new form of leisure received no small amount of attention given the fact that some early proponents included Henry Ford, Thomas Alva Edison, Harvey Firestone, and President Warren G. Harding—who not only camped but did so together as a group. Thanks in large part to the affordability of the automobile, a larger public would soon follow suit. By 1921, an estimated 20,000 people had driven across the country, and in the following year, the *New York Times* predicted that 5 million out of 10.8 million cars on the road would be used for camping.

Motor camping took many forms, from the crudest of tents to the tent trailer, the Gypsy Wagon to the handmade luxury Aerocar from aviation pioneer Glenn Curtiss (who had designed his own custom trailer back in 1919). The travel trailer not only made car camping cheaper and easier, it provided (nearly) all the comforts of home in a compact and transportable package. *Fortune* may have termed them a "really grand gadget for camping and vacation trips" in 1937, but trailers did make vacations possible for more people.

Whether their accommodations were jerry-rigged or custom-built, early autocampers embodied a new synthesis between the ideal of camping as a rustic, natural activity (popularized by Teddy Roosevelt) and the romantic notion of technology steering mankind into a comfortable but adventurous future.[1]

SETTING UP THE CAMP TRAILER
Pictured in the June 1935 issue of *Science Illustrated.* On the road the camp trailer is merely a welded aluminum box, but with the tent erected, it sleeps four comfortably. Courtesy of USC Special Collections.

1. Wallis, Allan D. *Wheel Estate: The Rise and Decline of Mobile Homes.* London: Oxford University Press, 1991, p. 32.

SEPTEMBER   35 CENTS

MOTOR CAMPER & TOURIST

Edited by R. W. DE MOTT

EXPERIMENTER PUBLISHING COMPANY, NEW YORK, PUBLISHERS OF
RADIO NEWS · SCIENCE & INVENTION · THE EXPERIMENTER · MOTOR CAMPER & TOURIST

MOTOR CAMPING BOOK (far left) Courtesy of Vintage Vacations.

CAMPING IN SEQUOIA NATIONAL PARK (left) Camping equipment by Western Auto Supply Company in 1931. Courtesy of USC Special Collections.

NASH CAMPING SET (above) This roof tent was available in 1949 as an option with a new Nash 600. Courtesy of Auto Club of Southern California Archive.

CAMPING SCENES (facing and above, top left)
Courtesy of USC Special Collections.

BUFFALO BILL'S HOME (above, bottom left) A tourist rendezvous
visited annually by thousands of cross-country visitors to North Platte,
Nebraska, 1931. Courtesy of USC Special Collections.

SECOND OUTING SHOW (top right) Western Auto Supply and
Motorola radios display their new products, 1928. Courtesy of Auto Club of
Southern California Archive.

CAMPING DISPLAY (bottom right) Models showing off the newest
camping equipment and how to use it, 1928. Courtesy of Auto Club of
Southern California Archive.

POP-UP UNITS Camping evolves from a simple shelter from the outdoors into the wonderfully compact pop-up camp unit that simply hitched to your car. The two images above were taken in Yosemite. Many different versions developed along the way, from hybrid pop-ups (above) to the literal home on wheels (left). Images courtesy of Phil Noyes.

KOZY *Coach*

TRADE NAME REG. U. S. PAT. OFF.

"FAVORITE OF THE ROAD-WISE"

Kozy Coach gives you everything you want for grand living in a small way. All steel electrically welded chassis prevents sagging, side-sway and assures quiet operation and perfect alignment. Write for free brochure to 409 E. Michigan Ave. Kalamazoo, Mich.

SEND FOR FREE CATALOG ★

KOZY COACH CO.

"You're Ahead with a Kozy Coach Behind"

RETIRE, RELAX Mr. and Mrs. Leslie Pearce enjoying their porch in Melbourne, Florida. Their community was sponsored by Chicago University and industrial firms to help solve the need for housing America's retired/retiring workforce. 1954. Courtesy of USC Special Collections.

If there is a common road down which all these vehicles have traveled, it is a dual highway of security and independence.

—"At Home on the Highway," Roger B. White, *American Heritage*, 1985

See Page 512

The more we get together, together, together
The more we get together, the happier we'll be.

—*Tin Can Tourists' official theme song*

PUT YOURSELF IN THIS PICTURE

The Federal De Luxe

FEDERAL

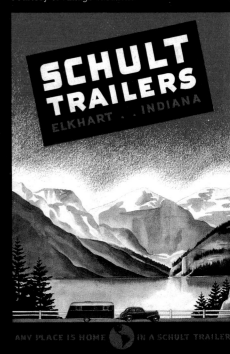

SCHULT
TRAILERS
ELKHART · · INDIANA

ANY PLACE IS HOME IN A SCHULT TRAILER

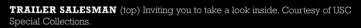

TRAILER SALESMAN (top) Inviting you to take a look inside. Courtesy of USC Special Collections.

CAR AND TRAILER SNAPSHOTS (above and right) Courtesy of Phil Noyes and Vintage Vacations.

Trailers in Camp
Orchard Beach
Manistee Mich
No 2

TRAILERS IN CAMP (lower left) Courtesy of USC Special Collections.

TRAILER PARK (facing, top left) Courtesy of Auto Club of Southern California Archive.

SNAPSHOTS (above and facing, bottom left) Assorted American trailerites.
Images courtesy of Vintage Vacations / Phil Noyes / Deke O'Malley.

CAMPGROUND ILLUSTRATION (facing, right) Courtesy of Vintage Vacations.

TRAILER PARK (above left) Santa Monica, California. Courtesy of USC Special Collections.

TRAILER PARK (above right) Laguna Beach, California. Courtesy of Auto Club of Southern California Archive.

TRAILERITES (above and left) Unique characters in front of their trailer, 1938. Courtesy of Marylou Kingsbury Stuart.

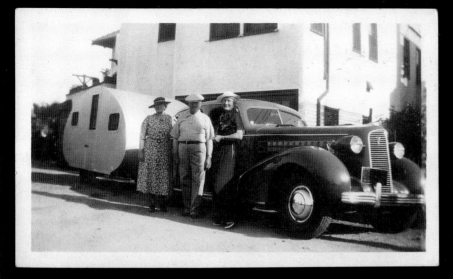

Daddy ♦ Lesel.

Arizona

Paul   1953

T.C.T — CAMP SARASOTA FLA — FEB — 8 — 1937 —

SNAPSHOTS Images courtesy of Vintage Vacations and Phil Noyes.

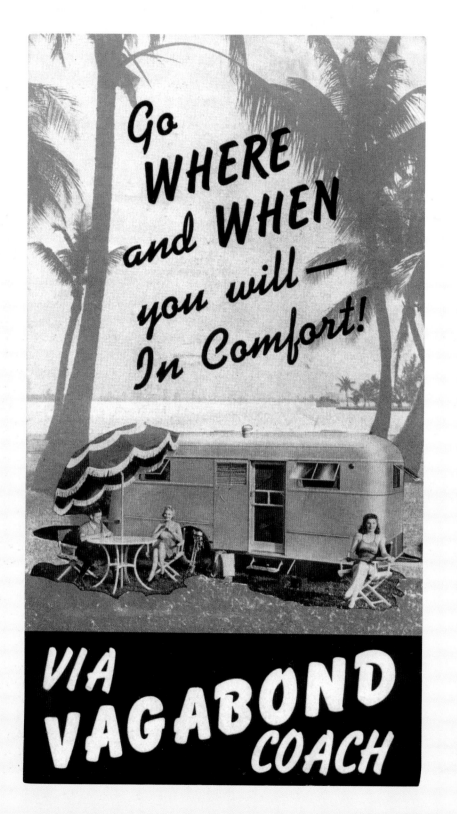

Go WHERE and WHEN you will— In Comfort!

VIA VAGABOND COACH

Go anywhere, stop anywhere, escape taxes and rent—this is irresistible.
Nothing but death has ever before offered so much in a single package.

—*AUTOMOTIVE INDUSTRIES*, DECEMBER 1936

SELLING THE DREAM

ADVERTISEMENTS AND PERIODICALS

BROCHURE IMAGERY
Collected on this page are common themes echoed in trailer advertisements: seeing the world yourself and finding a more fulfilled life in the process. This is possible with the conveniences of your modern trailer. Imagery from a Vagabond brochure, a Spartan illustration, and a Schult Coach illustrated letterhead. Materials courtesy of Vintage Vacations.

By 1937, close to 400 companies were building and selling trailers. The fierce competition resulting from this boom in production required the trailer industry to be extremely savvy with its marketing. Because the industry had yet to fully define itself—was it selling temporary housing? permanent homes? camping equipment?—its advertisements ran the gamut.

To appeal to those in the market for housing, companies conjured up images of home and hearth. Kozy Coach, for example, guaranteed a "'Home Sweet Home' Wherever You Roam," while another campaign equated trailer life with exceptional family values, suggesting that trailer living could enrich the lives of children by exposing them to the diversity of the American landscape. Many trailer companies offered more room and a dizzying array of modern conveniences such as "a kitchen to delight the most fastidious housewife." Other manufacturers aimed higher, attempting to equate trailers with luxury by throwing around words like royal, imperial, magnificent, even offering a *mansionette*. Armchair mechanics were lured in by ads providing information on the latest technological advances, from Terry's "tuck-away" Parking Hitch to a TORQ-LESS axle. Companies who saw travel as the linchpin of successful trailer sales promised their customers romance, freedom and unlimited adventure.

As trailers increased in popularity in the thirties, they became a topic covered by major publications, from *Popular Mechanics* to the *Saturday Evening Post.* Inevitably a spate of trailer-related periodicals emerged to cover the culture in-depth. Magazines like *Trail-R-News, Trailer Travel,* and *Automobile and Trailer Travel* offered tips on everything from hitches to a "Housekeeping on Wheels" column edited by The Trailer Wife. These periodicals were, of course, excellent vehicles for trailer and trailer-related product advertising, but perhaps most importantly, they helped to create a trailer community by providing a forum for passionate trailerites to share their experiences and information.

PROMOTIONAL MATERIALS

THE MOST SUCCESSFUL VEHICLE OF ITS KIND IN THE WORLD!

Correct! Fact is, there are more Dodge Motor Homes on the road today than all other vehicles of this type *combined*. The reasons for our remarkable success? First of all, the Dodge Motor Home was designed, from the wheels up, to be *exactly that*. We didn't convert a bus. We didn't stretch out a milk truck or tack four wheels and an engine onto a house trailer.

Travco Corporation, builder of the Dodge Motor Home, started with this design target: Create a vehicle that allows a family to travel in luxurious freedom. To eat, sleep and live on the move. A vehicle with spacious cooking *and* eating space. A vehicle with extraordinary amounts of closet and storage room, as well as complete toilet and shower facilities. A vehicle in a size easily handled by people who usually drive automobiles. A vehicle with sufficient power to travel at top legal speeds in town and on the freeway.

As you read this brochure, you will note we have included many items normally considered "optional" as standard equipment. Power brakes and power steering, automatic transmission, radio, clock, heater/defroster, fully-equipped kitchen, full bath, permanent double bed, to name just a few. We know what people need and want in this type of vehicle. We should—we have built more motor homes than all the others put together.

PILOT & NAVIGATOR on our plush flight deck. All-vinyl bucket seats swivel toward center.

POWER STEERING, power brakes, automatic transmission, heater/defroster are all standard.

TRAVEL LOUNGE with a view. Or dinette. Or double bed. Or coffee corner.

WHERE TO NEXT, DAD? Wherever your whim and the roads lead you. No schedules. No reservations. No setups or hookups. Just replenish your larder occasionally, and enjoy all your meals when you want them, where you want them. And, when it comes to driving, even the petite lady of the house enjoys a turn at the helm. (With power steering, automatic transmission, power brakes and a superb view of the road, what could be easier?)

ASSORTED BROCHURES All material in this section courtesy of Vintage Vacations, Phil Noyes, and Bryan Burkhart.

Two New
COVERED WAGON
Trailer Coaches
for . . .
1936

"Home Sweet Home"
Wherever You Roam

VIEW OF THE STANDARD MODEL

with THE KOZY COACH

Is there anything finer than to "get away from it all" now and then? Out along the water. Hunting through the woods. Tramping over the hills, or just lolling under the open sky. That's the life! Week ends, holidays and vacations spent in outdoor recreation and relaxation are not only enjoyable but necessary for healthful, zestful reserve on the job. But go in comfort, and economically—minus the sacrifices to hardships and inconveniences—minus the expense otherwise required for accommodations. And go to a new, a **different** spot whenever you wish, as leisurely as you like. Everybody's coming to it now. And everybody can, easily—with the wonderful KOZY COACH! There's a model (three in all) to suit anyone's purse or desires, as explained inside.

Pick Yours Now .

3 MODELS

• *DeLuxe*

• *Standard*

• *Junior*

the new way to spell smart living

PARAMOUNT / 1960

Silver St

"thirty"

America's Standard of
Trailer Coach Value for 1951

Star -Divisio
831 SOUTH

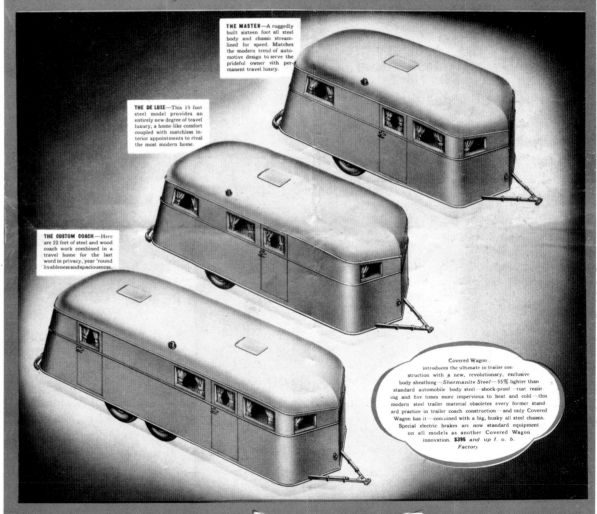

Announcing THREE NEW 1937
COVERED WAGON
TRAILER COACHES WITH EXCLUSIVE
SHERMANITE STEEL BODIES and STEEL CHASSIS

THE MASTER—A ruggedly built sixteen foot all steel body and chassi stream-lined for speed. Matches the modern trend of auto-motive design to serve the prideful owner with per-manent travel luxury.

THE DE LUXE—This 19 foot steel model provides an entirely new degree of travel luxury, a home-like comfort coupled with matchless in-terior appointments to rival the most modern home.

THE CUSTOM COACH—Here are 22 feet of steel and wood coach work combined in a travel home for the last word in privacy, year 'round livableness and spaciousness.

Covered Wagon introduces the ultimate in trailer con struction with a new, revolutionary, exclusive body sheathing—*Shermanite Steel*—55% lighter than standard automobile body steel—shock-proof—rust resist-ing and five times more impervious to heat and cold—this modern steel trailer material obsoletes every former stand ard practice in trailer coach construction—and only Covered Wagon has it—combined with a big, husky all steel chassis. Special electric brakes are now standard equipment on all models as another Covered Wagon innovation. **$395** *and up f. o. b. Factory*

COVERED WAGON

ORIGINATORS AND WORLD'S LARGEST BUILDERS OF TRAILER COACHES

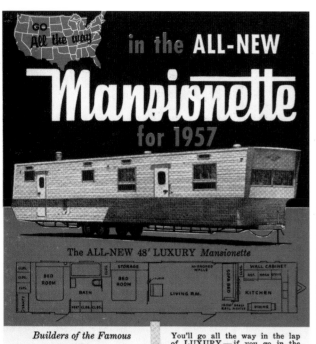

ful *1951*

F

uisers

A new and wonderful experience awaits you—the thrill of owning a new 1951 Kropf Cruiser . . . with incomparable beauty and styling throughout. You can now let your dreams come true in having the luxurious quality of a fine home in the finest of coaches—Kropf Cruisers. They're the coaches dealers are proud to sell and consumers proud to own.

The dignity and quiet beauty in clean, graceful lines— the perfect proportion in design—the profusion of color harmony—and the finest in materials and workmanship make Kropf Cruisers the greatest coaches ever. Write for literature.

Dealers: Write today for facts on dealerships available.

KROPF MANUFACTURING COMPANY
GOSHEN, INDIANA

Lovely to Look at ⋆

⋆ *Marvelous to Live in*

Introducing a New Era in

With *Every* Home Comfort

The Pullman Compartment Seats 5 or 6 At Meal Time

COVERED W

Luxurious Trailer Travel . . .

e

GON *for* 1936

A Kitchen to Delight the Most Fastidious Housewife

ARTHUR SHERMAN'S COVERED WAGON

14' 0"

BED SEAT
STORAGE

DINING
TABLE

PANTRY UNDER
STOVE

BED SEAT
STORAGE UNDER

STOVE
VENT

HEATING
STOVE

BUY DIRECT *from* **FACTORY**
and **SAVE!**

BED SEAT
STORAGE UNDER

SINK

DAVENPORT
STORAGE L

DINING
TABLE

STOVE

BED SEAT
STORAGE UNDER

STOVE
VENT

HEATING
STOVE

17' 2"

20'6"

WARDROBE

TOILET

Everywhere You Go!

SPARTAN

Homes Today 1953

The DETRO

The Motor City
Standard of Valu

Again... SCHULT LEADS
— WITH THE STUNNING NEW
Dwellavan

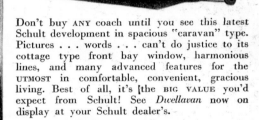

Don't buy ANY coach until you see this latest Schult development in spacious "caravan" type. Pictures . . . words . . . can't do justice to its cottage type front bay window, harmonious lines, and many advanced features for the UTMOST in comfortable, convenient, gracious living. Best of all, it's [the BIG VALUE you'd expect from Schult! See *Dwellavan* now on display at your Schult dealer's.

Free...

BIG, NEW, 8-PAGE ILLUSTRATED CATALOG ON BOTH SIZES OF THE SENSATIONAL HIGHER, ROOMIER *Dwellavan*. SEND A CARD OR LETTER TODAY TO DEPARTMENT 1808.

Beautifully decorated interiors, enhanced by *three* picture windows in the living room. Harmonizing drapes, upholstery and bordered linoleum.

★

The kitchen is a housewife's dream; so complete, and streamlined for convenience.

★

Rear bedrooms are luxurious; equipped with island beds and two chests, or twin beds and a single larger dresser.

SCHULT **SCHULT** *In Canada: H. B. McGinnis Co., Ltd., Peterborough, Ontario*

CORPORATION, ELKHART, INDIANA

The Magnificent

Imperial Spartanette

SPARTAN

It is a new way of life—a new way of life which will eventually change our architecture, our morals, our laws, our industrial system, and our system of taxation.

—*Harper's,* May 1937

MODERN LIVING

Early this century . . . .

A Horseless-carriage created a furore, challenging conservative people . . . But the Automobile is here to stay.

A Flying-machine was startling, and declared a freak . . . Now, many will travel no other way.

A Caravan conjured up romantic dreams of a carefree life — bright and gay.

Evolution manifests itself come-what-may, and proudly we present . . . . . .

"THE SPARTAN HOMES OF TODAY"

Your own home . . .
The popular Royal Spartanette

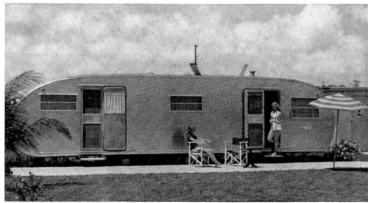

Go where the jobs pay best . . . live in easy-to-manage
and easy-to-keep-clean Spartan Homes

Easy monthly payments to suit your budget . . . own your
own home and pay like rent

National Automobile Show

Grand Central Palace, New York

PACE MAKER FOR AMERICAN INDUSTRY

NOV. 11-18, 1936

Luxurious
PAN-AMERICAN
★

THE PRODUCTION BUILT

TRAILER COACH WITH

CUSTOM·BUILT FEATURES

Have the time
of your life...
the
National
way

SPARTAN AIRCRAFT'S NEW, MODERN

Royal **SPARTANETTE**

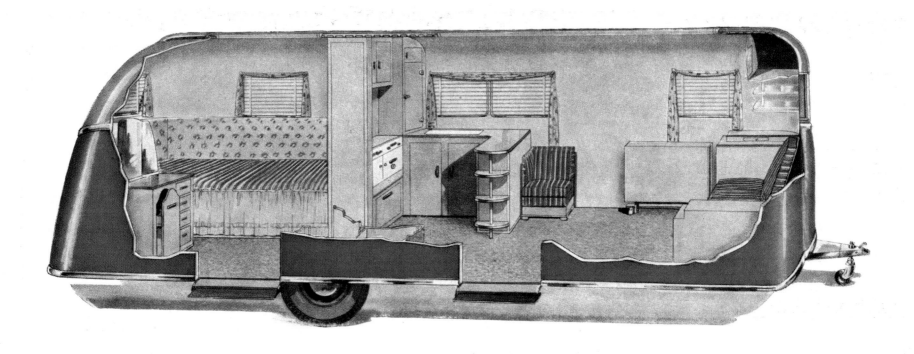

THE INTERIOR OF THE NEW **Palace** IS REFRESHINGLY ORIGINAL

The greatest advance in modern trailer travel!

AIRSTREAM for '54

LIGHTWEIGHT TRAVEL TRAILERS

SILVER DOME
for 1936

Motorized TRAVEL HOMES

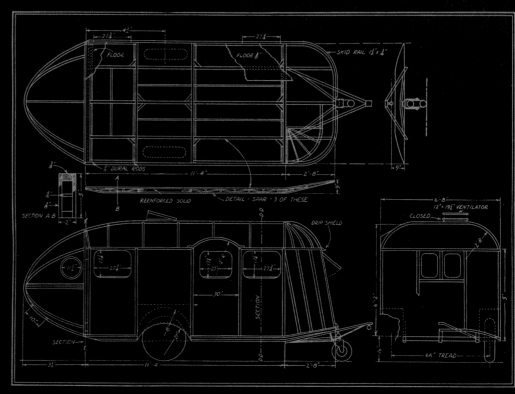

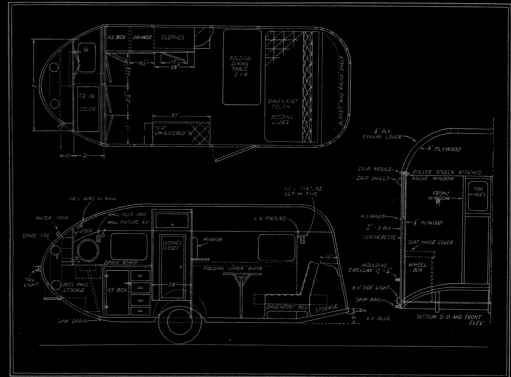

DO IT YOURSELF PLANS (above) From the February 1936 issue of *Home Craft* pictured on opposite page. Courtesy of Phil Noyes.

Popular HOME CRAFT

The Home Workshop Magazine

February – 1936

35¢

50¢ IN CANADA

Build This Trailer;
Roomy, economical, dependable.

BUILD IT YOURSELF

AUTOMOBILE and **Trailer Travel** MAGAZINE

MARCH, 1946

10 CENTS

IN THIS ISSUE

Cover	Constructive Discussions
Courtesy of Mr. H. J. McClellan	A New Department
Land of the Trembling Earth	The Greetings Exchange
By Dorothy Y. Glick	Housekeeping on Wheels
Over Night Stops	Mail Bag
By Major R. E. Edwards	Industry News
	Trailer Parks

THE OLDEST AND LARGEST TRAILER PUBLICATION

25¢

TRAILER TRAVEL

JANUARY, 1957

. . . In This Issue . . .

- They Pursue Opportunity
- Florida Show Report
- Tackle Your Refurbishes Easy
- Yesterday's Children

OLDEST MAGAZINE FOR MOBILE HOME LIVING

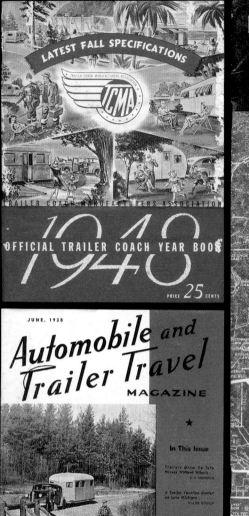

LATEST FALL SPECIFICATIONS

TCMA
TRAILER COACH MANUFACTURERS ASSOCIATION

TRAILER COACH MANUFACTURERS ASSOCIATION

1948

OFFICIAL TRAILER COACH YEAR BOOK

PRICE **25** CENTS

JUNE, 1938

Automobile and Trailer Travel
MAGAZINE

★

In This Issue

Trailers Grow Up Into
Houses Without Wheels . . .
E. C. FRANKLIN

A Trailer Vacation Center
on Lake Michigan . . .
WALTER WINTER

Seeing the West Coast . . .
EDISON R. HARRIS

Are You Also Towing an
Unseen Trailer? . . .
FREDERICK C. RUSSELL

20¢

THE MAGAZINE OF MOTORIZED TRAVEL IN AMERICA

Trail·R·News Magazine
THE COMPLETE MOBILE HOME

DECEMBER 1954 • 20c

The only American magazine
whose editors live and travel
in trailers.

Palm Springs Rally

Grandma and Mobile Living

Hurricane Hazel Strikes Trailerists

SAN DIEGO TRAILER SUPPLY
6881 El Cajon Blvd.
San Diego 15, California

The Highway Traveler

AIRSTREAM

LLANFAIRPWLLGWYNGYCHGOGERICHYRNDROBWYLLLLATISILLOGOGCGOCH *IN* NORTH

TUTTGART	FLORENCE	PARIS	ALASSIO	DOVER
MUNICH	PISA	VICHY	DIANA MARINA	LONDON
BERLIN	GENOA	BIARITZ	JUAN-LES-PINS	SOUTHAI
VIENNA	MONTE CARLO	ANTIBES	LYONS	CARDIFF
ZURICH	NICE	STRASBOURG	AMIENS	BIGGLES
LUCERNE	CANNES	FONTAINBLEU	DUNKIRK	LEEDS
LUGANO	COVIGLIAIO	NAPLES	AVIGNON	NEWCAST
MILAN	BOLOGNA	LIVORNO	NEUILLY	BIRMING
VENICE	ROVIGO			

Believe me, there is no way to see and know the world as you can traveling by trailer. We are already looking forward to next year's expedition. Mind you, this one hasn't even ended, and we're thinking about the next!

—WALLY BYAM, *TRAILER TRAVEL HERE AND ABROAD,* 1960

WISH YOU WERE HERE

DISPATCHES FROM THE ROAD

Almost as important as traveling the world was letting the folks back home know where you'd been and what you'd seen. Postcards have long been an essential part of the tourist experience, no less so for trailerites. Nearly every trailer company and trailer park from Portland, Oregon, to Sarasota, Florida, produced a commemorative postcard—typically a rather banal photographic image printed on linen. Also popular were comic illustrations of trailer travel—bawdy and colorful depictions of situations most often involving partially clad women or outhouses.

Many trailer aficionados took the postcard one step further by writing personal narratives of their travel experiences. Favorite discoveries, trip highlights, mechanical difficulties, and the frustrations that come with being in an unfamiliar place were all recounted with enthusiasm and descriptive detail. Perhaps the most famous of these travelers' tales is Wally Byam's *Trailer Travel Here and Abroad,* in which the charismatic founder of Airstream bolsters his legend with tales of travels throughout North America, Europe, Africa and the Middle East. *Folding Bedouins or Adrift in a Trailer* tells the story not of wandering nomads in Africa but of newspaper reporter Howard Vincent O'Brien's family vacation in a trailer in 1936.

For the most part, these books offered a quirky mix of memoir, travelogue, and practical how-to advice. Similar to the trailer postcards, these volumes helped bring the world of trailer travel to the armchair travelers back home.

POSTCARDS FROM THE ROAD (above)

MOST TRAVELED TRAILER (facing) Owned by Wally Byam, the founder of Airstream, Inc., Byam led trailer caravans all over the world and generated noteworthy press along the way (note the North Wales town with 57 letters in the name!),1951. Courtesy of USC Special Collections.

I CAN'T BEAR TO BE PARTED FROM YOU...
I WISH YOU'D TRAIL ALONG!

We didn't know whether for this year's vacation
To buy us an auto or boat,
So we go by auto, but when we come to water
We just set our trailer afloat.

SWIMIN'-HOME

HAVING OUR UPS AND DOWNS BUT
WE'RE REALLY GOING
PLACES

TRAIL ALONG TO TRAILER TOWN

If you didn't like your town and you moved
All connections you could drop
But now if your town is all on the move
When you want to move you stop!

THIS LIFE SURE MAKES ONE FEEL YOUNG!

"IF HE ONLY KNEW WHAT WAS COMING!"

19

23

"WILFRED, THAT HITCH-HIKER WE GAVE A LIFT TO — HE'S GETTING FRESH!"

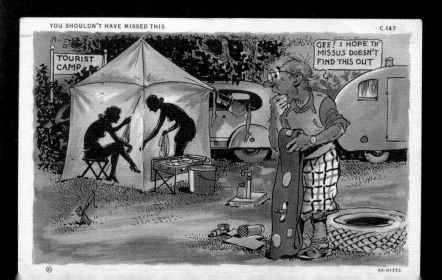

YOU SHOULDN'T HAVE MISSED THIS

C.147

TOURIST CAMP

GEE! I HOPE TH' MISSUS DOESN'T FIND THIS OUT

6A-H1773

SEEING NATURE IN THE RAW IS A WONDERFUL THING!

LOOKING FORWARD FOR BETTER TIMES—

ALL ABOARD - LETS GO

Greetings from Hale, Mich.

PG-7—Municipal Trailer Park, Punta Gorda, Fla.

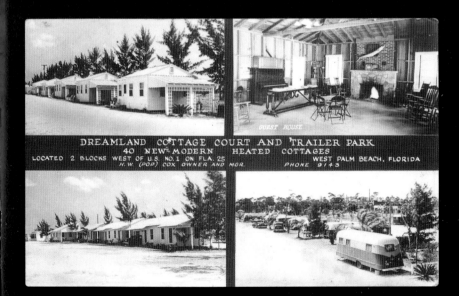

GUEST HOUSE

DREAMLAND COTTAGE COURT AND TRAILER PARK
40 NEW-MODERN HEATED COTTAGES
LOCATED 2 BLOCKS WEST OF U.S. NO.1 ON FLA. 25   WEST PALM BEACH, FLORIDA
H.W. (POP) COX OWNER AND MGR.   PHONE 9143

A Trailer Camp in Florida   189

BRYAN TRAILER SALES
½ Mile East of Bryan, Ohio

Alto Trailer Sales
3320 Airline Highway (U. S. 51-61-65) New Orleans, La.

Bradbury Trailer Sales
U. S. Hwy. 1, West Peabody, Mass.

BRADBURY TRAILER SALES
SPARTAN
TRAILER Coaches

Village Green Trailer Sales
U. S. 322 and Pa. 452
Village Green, Pa.

Village Green Trailer Park

Village Green Swimming Pool

S-67—Tropical Living in Sarasota Trailer Park
Sarasota, Fla.

PORTLAND TRAILER COURT. ON U.S. 99. PORTLAND. ORE.

A Modern Trailer Park   In St. Petersburg, Florida

OB-H1524

Trailer Camp, Municipal Lakeside Park,
Seneca Lake, Watkins Glen, N. Y.
In the Finger Lakes Region

South on Rolling Wheels

TRAILER ADVENTURES IN THE SOUTH

Ann Brooks

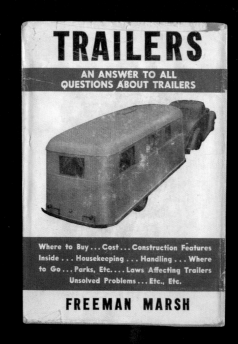

TRAILERS

AN ANSWER TO ALL
QUESTIONS ABOUT TRAILERS

Where to Buy...Cost...Construction Features
Inside...Housekeeping...Handling...Where
to Go...Parks, Etc....Laws Affecting Trailers
Unsolved Problems...Etc., Etc.

FREEMAN MARSH

FOLDING BEDOUINS

OR ADRIFT IN A TRAILER

HOWARD VINCENT O'BRIEN

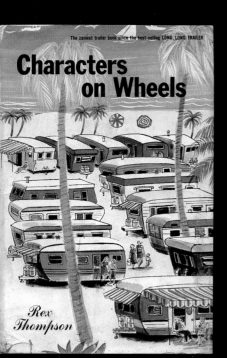

The zaniest trailer book since the best-selling LONG, LONG TRAILER

Characters on Wheels

Rex Thompson

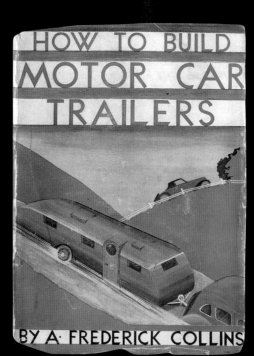

HOW TO BUILD MOTOR CAR TRAILERS

BY A. FREDERICK COLLINS

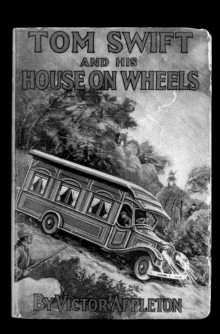

TOM SWIFT AND HIS HOUSE ON WHEELS

BY VICTOR APPLETON

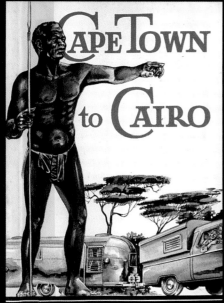

Cape Town to Cairo

Lillie B. Douglass

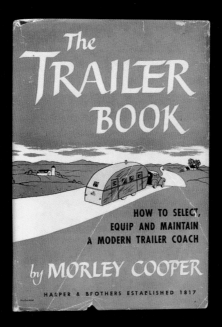

The TRAILER BOOK

HOW TO SELECT, EQUIP AND MAINTAIN A MODERN TRAILER COACH

by MORLEY COOPER

HARPER & BROTHERS ESTABLISHED 1817

HOLIDAY IN A TRAILER

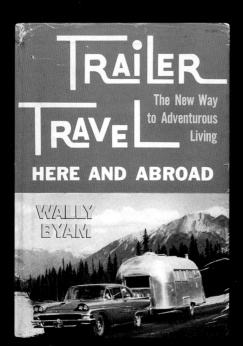

TRAILER TRAVEL

The New Way to Adventurous Living

HERE AND ABROAD

WALLY BYAM

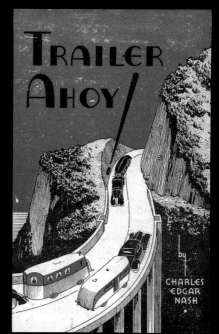

TRAILER AHOY

by CHARLES EDGAR NASH

The FOLLETT PICTURE-STORY of

THE TALE OF A TRAILER

FOLLETT PUBLISHING COMPANY · CHICAGO

Five years ago, it was just a convenience for motor tourists . . . a mobile bedroom dragged along behind the car. Today it is a fairly complete home, factory-built and it is the only home of thousands of Americans who have gone gypsy.

—*THE NEW YORK TIMES MAGAZINE*, NOVEMBER 1, 1936

TRAILER SHOWS

KEEPING AN EYE ON THE NEW CURVES

In *Trailer Ahoy!* Charles Edgar Nash recounted his experience on the trailer-show circuit in 1937: "Trailers were shown in every automobile show of any size this year and in every case they literally 'stole the show' by admission of the automobile men themselves. Interested visitors and prospective purchasers swarmed around the trailers, examining every little detail of their design and construction. For some this was a first intimate contact with a trailer."

Indeed, trailer shows were veritable playgrounds for legions of trailer-tappers (those who rapped on the door to ask for a look inside) and serious paying customers alike. The public, it seemed, couldn't get enough of these "homes on wheels." When the spectator grew weary of the latest in body types or hitches, other distractions were on tap—most notably, women. Beauty pageants were staples of trailer shows (though in the interest of gender equality, one auto-show review in *Trailer Life* reported on a most beautiful leg contest for the men. Incidentally, that same venue also sponsored a competition for Most Glamorous Grandma.)

The undeniable appeal of short-skirted ingenues notwithstanding, the primary function of these events was to introduce the latest innovations and gadgets to a willing and enthusiastic audience. As one industry observer put it, back in 1955, "Manufacturers attempt to provide everything Mr. and Mrs. Trailerite might desire—even to the point of pampering them."

THE SHOW OF ALL SHOWS (left) The Third Outing Trailer Show in 1936 took place in a picturesque courtyard setting and presented some of the most stylish new trailers of the decade. Courtesy of Auto Club of Southern California Archive.

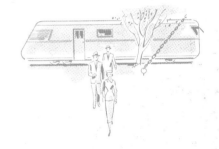

COURTYARD VIEW (facing) A view of the Third Outing Trailer Show in 1936, sponsored by the TCAA (Trailer Coach Association of America). The two trailers (bottom center) with small billboards in front are a Glider and a Hollywood Nomad. Courtesy of Auto Club of Southern California Archive.

THE LONG, LONG TRAILER (top) The title of the novel by Clinton Twiss and a popular film starring Desi Arnaz and Lucille Ball, this trailer was displayed at the first annual Trailer Life Show in 1954. It was manufactured by Airfloat Trailer-coaches. Courtesy of USC Special Collections.

GO GO GO (left) To the first annual Trailer Life Show, sponsored by the TCAA, 1954. Original photographs complete with airbrush work for newspaper printing. Courtesy of USC Special Collections.

MISS TRAILER LIFE (left) Actress Joyce Holden sitting in chair, is crowned in preparation for the opening of the second annual Trailer Life Show in the Great Western Exhibit Hall, 1955. Courtesy of USC Special Collections.

EIGHTH OUTING SHOW Howard F. Ward trailer display, 1941.

TRAILER GIRLS Trailer dealers understood the need to have not only attractive trailers on the lot or at the show, but attractive ladies, too. Courtesy of Delmar Watson.

TRAILER FAMILY (facing) Getting the word out for the big show. Courtesy of Delmar Watson.

MORE THAN JUST TRAILERS (facing) A well-timed photograph as onlookers hold their breath as the ski-jump daredevil soars in mid-flight. Courtesy of Delmar Watson.

SCENES FROM THE SHOW (above) A sea of wondrous forms and shapes. Courtesy of Delmar Watson.

These [trailer dwellers] are Martians. I wanted to ask them to take me to their leader. They have no humor, no past, and their future is new models . . .

—John Steinbeck, EXPLAINING WHY HE BOUGHT A TRUCK INSTEAD OF A TRAILER, 1960

PANORAMIC VIEW of Trailer Village. Courtesy of Delmar Watson.

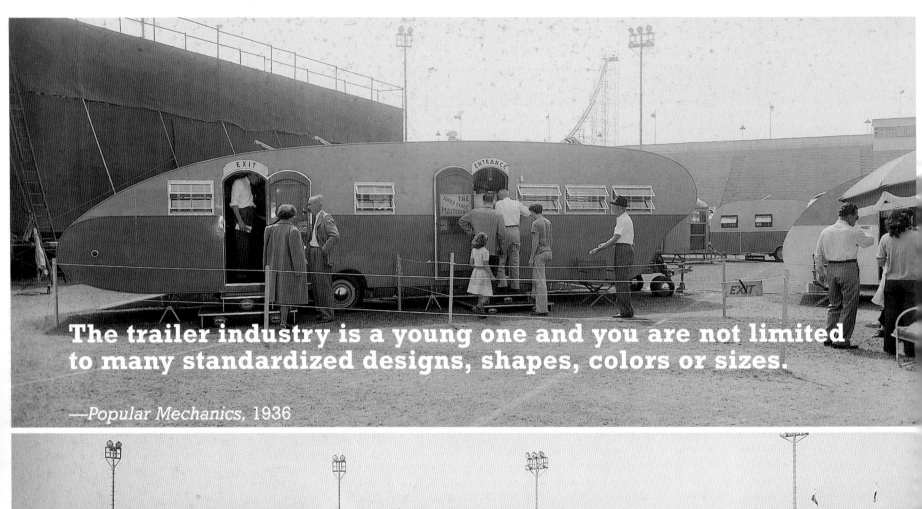

The trailer industry is a young one and you are not limited to many standardized designs, shapes, colors or sizes.

—*Popular Mechanics*, 1936

BOWLUS DISPLAY AT THE TRAILER SHOW, 1935. Courtesy of Auto Club of Southern California Archive.

The trailer is a hybrid of the aeroplane, automobile and house in construction and engineering.

—Trailer Topics, June 1940

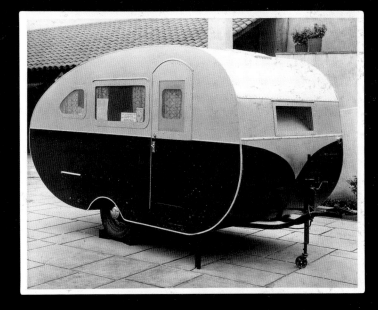

AIRSTREAM TRAILER DISPLAY (above and right) Courtesy of Auto Club of Southern California Archive.

THIRD OUTING TRAILER SHOW (top), 1936. Courtesy of Auto Club of Southern California Archive.

AIRFLOAT TRAILER AND A CHRYSLER AIRFLOW SEDAN (above), 1936. Courtesy of Auto Club of Southern California Archive.

TRAVEL OME LIMITED (above) The deluxe model at the Second Outing Trailer Show, 1935. Courtesy of Auto Club of Southern California Archive.

They are very popular with hunters.
College students are living in them.
In fact the scope of their use is limited
only by the ingenuity of their owners.

—*Trailer Ahoy,* 1937

A GABLE-LIKE POSE (top left)
A dandy posing with his Cadillac LaSalle
pulling a Travel Ome trailer, 1935.
Courtesy of Auto Club of Southern
California Archive.

ANOTHER VIEW (above)
1935. Courtesy of Auto Club of Southern
California Archive.

AIRFLOAT TRAILER (left) At the
Third Outing Trailer Show, 1936.
Courtesy of Auto Club of Southern
California Archive.

KIT TRAILER and girl. Courtesy of Delmar Watson.

AIRSTREAM TRAILER and girl. Courtesy of Delmar Watson.

NORTH DAKOTA (top right) Two women chat in front of a Hollywood Nomad trailer, 1936. Courtesy of Auto Club of Southern California Archive.

TRAILER SALES (right) Syd Smith Trailer Sales. Culver City, California, 1947. Courtesy of Auto Club of Southern California Archive.

AIRFLOAT DISPLAY (facing) A stylish group poses with the 1936 new Airfloat. Courtesy of Auto Club of Southern California Archive.

TAKE A LOOK INSIDE

HEY, THIS IS REALLY NICE . . .

AIRSTREAM CLIPPER (left) Trailer-show patrons sneak a peek into the exquisite trailer's interior. At the Second Outing Trailer Show, 1936. Courtesy of Auto Club of Southern California Archive.

ADVERTISEMENT (above) for Liberty Mobile Homes. Courtesy of Vintage Vacations.

Like old-fashioned Easter eggs that enclose complex and colorful dioramas sculpted from sugar or the majestic sailing ships captured in narrow-mouthed glass bottles, trailer interiors are a delight to behold—and are a bit of a mystery for the beholder. How do all those components manage to fit into such a small space?

The trailer—a perfect, self-contained unit for living—is truly a masterpiece of design, engineering and construction. The best examples were developed by naturally curious (and slightly obsessed) innovators like Glenn Curtiss, Arthur Sherman, and William Hawley Bowlus, men fascinated with the challenge of how to fit icebox, bed, bath, sink, storage space, and more, into a predetermined amount of space. For them, a lack of square footage was not an obstacle but a welcome challenge, a creative and intellectual problem to solve. In the resulting products, form and function worked seamlessly together and each resolution as it came—aha! that's where I'll put the heater!—must truly have been a cause for celebration.

Trailers are, for most, all about outward appearances: a streamlined flash of silver heading down the highway (or perhaps a square-shaped monolith holding up traffic on the interstate). For the uninitiated who peer in to take a gander at a trailer's interior, the initial response is generally one of amazement, especially if one was lucky enough to be invited in to take a look at one of the classics, lovingly restored to its original condition. Trailers may have gotten larger—and larger—as satellite TV and microwaves have become de rigueur in one's home away from home but that golden age ingenuity has not been completely lost. One can still marvel at the complexity of systems and structures that make up these unique vacation homes on wheels.

The only trouble is that, according to trailer "addicts," once you live in a home on wheels, you're never satisfied to be anchored to a permanent one again.

—*Popular Mechanics,* 1937

MODEL SHOOT (facing) A trio of beauties seated inside a Bowlus travel trailer, 1936. Courtesy of Auto Club of Southern California Archives.

INVITING INTERIOR (above) A model and a trailer on display at the 1950 Sportsmen's Vacation and Trailer Show at the Gilmore Stadium. Courtesy of USC Special Collections.

MODEL SHOOT (facing, top left) Two models and a cute puppy relax in the trailer's dinner area. Courtesy of Auto Club of Southern California Archive.

SPACIOUS INTERIOR (facing, bottom left) Glenn Sanders relaxing inside his new 1955 Rocket 27-foot trailer manufactured by Silver Streak Trailer Company in El Monte, California. Silver Streak used an all-metal airplane-type construction, while the interior material consisted of natural wood veneer cabinets, select use of laminate counters and lush period upholstery and fabrics. Courtesy of USC Special Collections.

BUNK BEDS AND A BIRTHDAY! (left and above) Denny Watson, 5, Johnny Roberts, 5, and Leslie Roberts, 6-1/2, clown around on the trailer's bunk beds and celebrate a birthday. As trailer size expanded, so did their ability to comfortably accommodate the children and their friends on the holiday. Courtesy of Delmar Watson.

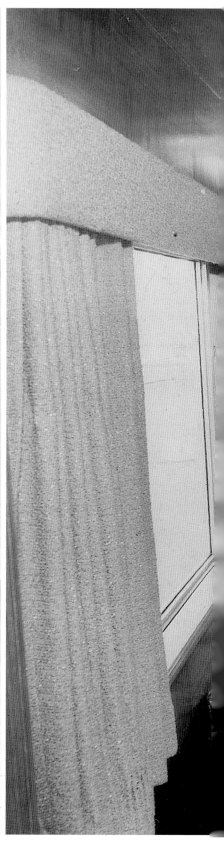

NEW PATTERN IN AMERICAN LIVING (above) Another modern trailer, rivaling the modern apartment in utility and beauty, the trailer also expedited a solution to temporary housing shortages as war workers returned home, 1951. Courtesy of USC Special Collections.

YOU DESERVE THE BEST (right) This cozy interior awaits you in this luxurious 65-foot "Executive Flagship" revealed at the Trailer Life Show in 1954. Yours for a mere $75,000. Courtesy of Delmar Watson.

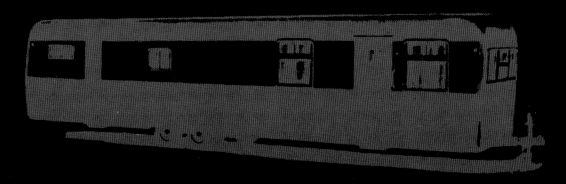

For full-time living purposes, no trailer is too big.

—*Westways,* April 1950

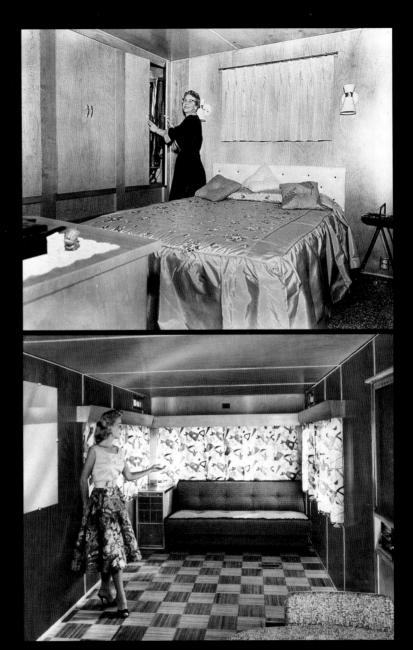

BEDROOM (top) Interior view of mobile home. Courtesy of Delmar Watson.
TRAVELMASTER (above) Interior view of mobile home. Courtesy of Vintage Vacations.
LIBERTY MOBILE HOME (facing) Illustration courtesy of Vintage Vacations.

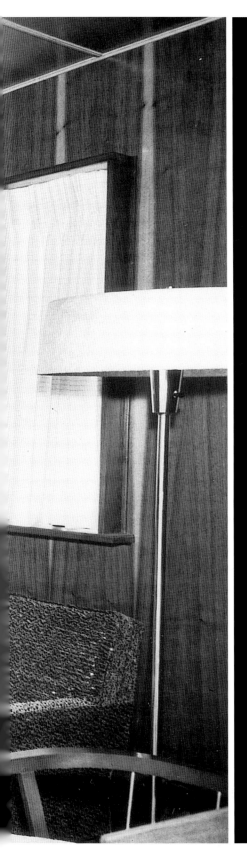

WARMING UP TO THE MOBILE HOME (above) Saucy Carole Campbell heats her hands on an oil burner in one of the 1959 models shown at the Los Angeles Trailer Show. Courtesy of USC Special Collections.

MOBILE HOME (facing) It has wheels but usually they don't move very much. Courtesy of Delmar Watson.

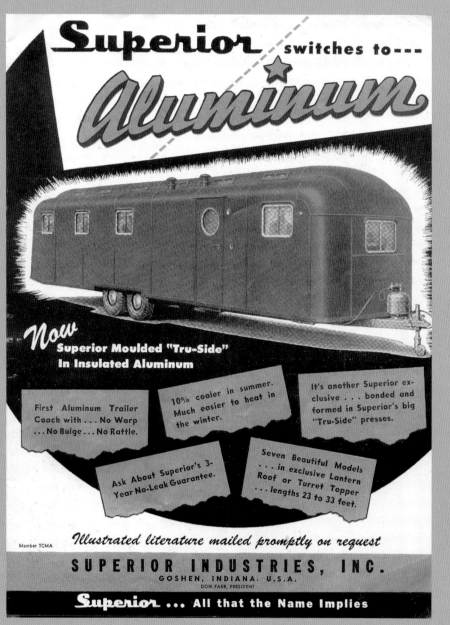

SUPERIOR BROCHURE (above) Courtesy of Phil Noyes.

CANE CHAIRS (right) Inside a new trailer at the ACSC headquarters garage.
Courtesy of Auto Club of Southern California Archive.

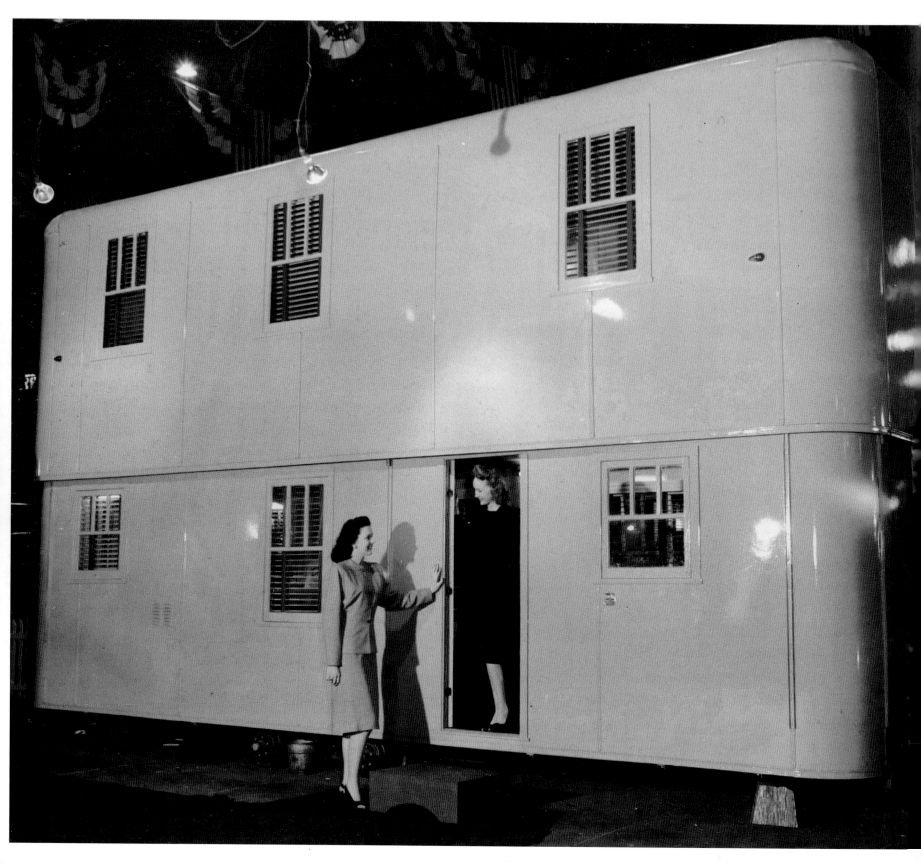

Let's not make any changes—let's make only improvements.

—WALLY BYAM

I'VE GOT THIS IDEA

DEVELOPMENTS ALONG THE WAY

LARK HOUSEBOAT (above) Trailer design ventures into friendly waters. Courtesy of USC Special Collections.

TWO STORIES HIGH AND PORTABLE (left), 1946. Liberty Trailercoaches boldly presents a larger family model that extrudes to accommodate six persons in a five-room, two-story home. It was displayed at the National Trailer Coach Show in Chicago, Illinois. Lynne Walker (left) and Billie Sellers stand at the main entrance. The upper story is raised and lowered by hydraulic lifts. When collapsed, it measures 11 feet high. Raised with wheels demounted, it is 15-1/2 feet high. Courtesy of USC Special Collections.

On the surface, a trailer would seem to be a fairly standardized structure. Few objects, however, have become the focus of such compulsive tweaking, tinkering and fine-tuning. From the beginning the trailer has, for its inventors and owners, been an obsession—something to be continuously improved, refined, refinished. These men were seemingly inspired by industrial designer Raymond Loewy's oft-repeated declaration to "Never leave well enough alone."

Arthur Sherman was an exemplar of these industrious, often entrepreneurial men who had a vision for what trailers could be. In 1928, after a frustrating experience assembling an expensive tent trailer he'd purchased, Sherman went home to design and build his own trailer. The masonite clunker wasn't pretty but it was durable, and unlike a tent trailer, no assembly was required. After a stranger offered to buy it from him, he sold and built some more, and before long, a company—Sherman's Covered Wagons—was born.

Indeed, by the thirties, so many companies and individuals like Sherman were working on their own personal vision for trailers that the industry became an exemplar of design innovation. As the decade progressed and the number of companies and individuals experimenting with form, technology and structure tapered off, the more sound advances and innovations—like William Hawley Bowlus's streamlined shell, for example—prevailed, while wildly impractical schemes like the five-room duplex apartment masquerading as a two-story trailer designed by Corwin Willson had a deservedly short life span.

By the end of the thirties, trailers began to expand in weight, width and length to accommodate the gadgets and inventions that proliferated modern life. In many cases they served as permanent homes. The excitement that designers like Glenn Curtiss had felt trying to fit all the comforts of home in one small package dissipated as trailers grew—and grew. But the desire of trailer owners to modernize their propane system, replace loose rivets, or polish a skin 'til it gleams has never wavered.

111

THE AEROCAR (facing) Glenn Curtiss's "motor bungalow" was described as a compact hotel on wheels. Curtiss was a maverick inventor and designer. Along with his successful line of trailers in the twenties, Curtiss manufactured the Jenny airplane, the flying boat and a motorcycle that bore his name. Courtesy of Phil Noyes.

BUILD YOUR OWN (above right) Advertisement prompting people to buy plans and build their own trailer. Courtesy of Phil Noyes.

AN EARLY HOUSE TRAILER (above right) Postcard image courtesy Phil Noyes.

MORE THAN MEETS THE EYE (right) Bathing beauties, from left, Dolores Berriezo, Betty Koch and Connie James, demonstrate the expansion features of the "Expando-Home" at a trailer show. With a simple turn of a winch it doubles in width "within minutes." Courtesy of USC Special Collections.

THE CHL2 (left) Something new in habitats: a unique motorbus apartment used by an American tourist on the French Riviera. This house on wheels comes complete with style and every convenience. Photographed in Paris, France, 1926. Courtesy of USC Special Collections.

LONG, MAYBE THE LONGEST HOUSE TRAILER (above) At a cost of $5,000, this trailer was built for fourteen UCLA students to study, vacation and tour northern California, Oregon and Washington in 1935. The trailer was 34 feet long and 8 feet wide. The trip was arranged to promote UCLA to its northern neighbors. Featured within the trailer are showers, a kitchen, sleeping accommodations and an electric refrigerator. Courtesy of USC Special Collections.

THE AERO CABANA

Very little is known about this pop-up design, but not because it lacks merit. In the twenties and thirties, many of the tent and trailer manufacturers began building prototypes after hours in small backyard shops in hopes of developing a sound manufacturable product. The Aero Cabana relied on a small number of parts, which, once assembled, created an aerodynamic form that easily mounted to an automobile's roof gutters. This early-fifties design preceded the well-known Volkswagen pop-up roof tent. Images courtesy of Phil Noyes.

117

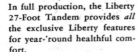

In full production, the Liberty 27-Foot Tandem provides *all* the exclusive Liberty features for year-'round healthful comfort.

LIBERTY
Introduced "Comfort Conditioning"

Including the Famous Three-Decker Heated Floor

NOW—in Liberty models—built-in "comfort conditioning," with the patented three-decker heated floor and circu-vent roof, assures positive floating air circulation summer and winter. For utmost comfort, enjoyment and health, insist upon the five basic Liberty features: effective insulation to neutralize heat and cold; an automatically heated floor; thorough circulation without drafts; complete, constant air change throughout the interior; a steady flow of fresh air, but with the exclusion of rain, snow and dust.

LIBERTY
Originated the Two-Story Portable Home with Five Rooms

and NOW

One of the most sensational developments in trailer coach history, the Liberty two-story portable home is provoking nationwide curiosity. "Comfort conditioned" throughout, it provides complete accommodations for a large family.

LIBERTY SETS THE PACE WITH "COMFORT CONDITIONING"

The Home of Your Dreams

Summer Evening Rendezvous
Warm and sunny during the day—delightfully cool at night—your sun porch will be a favorite spot for relaxing.

Toasty Warm in Winter
Substitute storm windows for screens and your sun porch adds another room to your already spacious mobile home.

Traveling Is Fun, and Easy
Fold the collapsible sun porch and side awnings against the coach and you have a 28'8" compact mobile unit.

Complete and Efficient
In front, with cross ventilation, is a modern kitchen with Frigidaire, bottled gas stove and double stainless steel sink.

Spacious and Livable
A handy drop-leaf table gives you ample room to serve six, can be closed to enlarge living room when dinner is over.

Sleeps Four—Maybe More
Inner door bed and studio couch make two full sized beds which can be separated at night by folding doors.

LOVELY TO LOOK AT . . . An attractive screened-in porch and large domestic-type windows with gay shutters make the Sun Coach a dream cottage to be proud of.

Member Trailer Coach Manufacturers Association

ELCAR Sun Coach

PRODUCT OF ELCAR COACH CORPORATION   831 South Wabash Ave., Dept. S-411, Chicago 5, Illinois

ELCAR SUN COACH AND LIBERTY ADVERTISEMENTS (facing left and above) Courtesy of Vintage Vacations.

PRETTY GULLIVER IN TRAILER TOWN (left) Sylvia Morrison examines a tiny trailer town–a 12 x 16-foot model of a projected trailer village near Santa Anita Park in Los Angeles, California, in 1946. The 55-acre project with a $300,000 price tag was backed by the nonprofit Trailer Coach Association of California. It contained 1,100 units and was designed so that four trailers made up each residential block. Courtesy of USC Special Collections.

One thing is sure—there is no monotony to life in a trailer.

—Folding Bedouins or Adrift in a Trailer, 1937

BLINK YOUR EYES IN DISBELIEF (above and facing) The Executive Cruiser by Mid States Corporation. Sixty-five feet rolling down the highway clearly redefines the concept of "King of the Road." It comes complete with sun deck, portable swimming pool (into which a model is about to dive from the trailer's springboard), solarium, bar, wine cellar, wall safe, moving-picture screen, radio, telephone, air conditioning and a few other extras, including a special helicopter landing strip on the roof. In 1954, this unit cost $75,000 and was displayed at the Trailer Life Show in the Shrine Exposition Hall. Courtesy of USC Special Collections.

The trailer owner is really a smart man; he is pioneering a new way of living.

—Trailer Topics, 1938

EARLY HOME-BUILT MOTOR HOME What more could you ask for? J. Roy Hunt holds open the door of his motor home to invite you in. Within are all the comforts of a small apartment plus a television, a complete 10-meter radio station, and a broadcast receiver. Hunt, a motion-picture camera man, constructed this self-propelled trailer home from 1942 in his spare time. Courtesy of USC Special Collections.

THE HUNT HOUSE CAR built by J. Roy Hunt in 1942 was the closest relative to the two Bowlus Motorchief housecars built between 1934 and 1936. Hunt was said to have built five or six of these great streamlined cars: the first, called the Turtle, completed in 1939, was built on a Ford chassis and had the engine in front. Next, Hunt built a rear steam-engine pusher at the then-exorbitant cost of $29,000. Then in 1942, he built another one, the "Miss Sheila Hollywood," named after his daughter, Sheila Hunt. Courtesy of USC Special Collections.

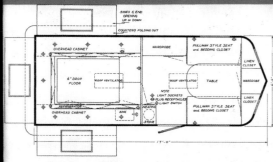

The Ideal Combination

The floor plan illustrates how you work in the rear of the coach, and live in the forward compartment. These two rooms are divided by a sliding door. Each is adequately equipped with such items as are essential to your comfort and well being.

Of course, it is of Schult roadable construction, built to render years and years of highly satisfactory service. Be sure to investigate it carefully, and be the first in your community, or with your show, to cash in on the profit opportunities it offers.

The picture to the left shows a Concession Vendor designed for a purveyor of barbecues, lettering and awnings were built to his special order. (Ordinarily the sides of the coach lift up to form a canopy rather than down as in this case.)

Below is a closeup of the living compartment showing the dinette (makes double bed) wardrobe, etc.

HAPPINESS AHEAD

The wonderful Schult Concession Vendor is in use all over the country helping men and women earn a good living doing interesting and easy work. These people find it an investment that really pays big dividends. They live a life of freedom—are their own bosses—and can follow the sunshine like the birds. There's happiness, profit and health ahead for Vendor owners.

Below picture shows part of the vending compartment.

BIG PROFITS AWAIT YOU

There are thousands of dollars profit awaiting the concession men who adapt the Schult Vendor to their business needs. Not only in savings over the old expensive method of packing and unpacking at each stand, but in the wonderful advertising and appearance value it will give you.

In addition to savings in dollars and cents and profits, there is much saved in labor, for when you're through on a location with your Concession Vendor you simply let down the sides, fold it up, put your equipment away, and you're ready to go to bed in the living compartment of the coach. Take it anywhere you want to go, your store and your home is always with you. It is a "natural" for concession folks. (There are hundreds of uses for it in other locations beside the shows, circuses and carnivals, one in your own community perhaps, a beach or highway junction, picnic ground or ball park.)

SPECIFICATIONS

Dimensions—17' by 6' 3" wide, by 6' 1" high - - - ALL STEEL CHASSIS and steel roof construction - - - *Body and Cabinets*—Especially selected fir plywood inside and outside, oak and fir joists, stringers, steel reinforcements - - - *Top*—Water proofed pre-shrunk decking aluminum painted - - - *Window*—Living quarters—1 large opening window on each side, window in door, 2 windows in front - - - *Vending Compartment*—Both sides, and end opening to form canopy - - - *Finish*—Living quarters—Natural fir finish, with light contrasting trim, vending compartment pure white enamel throughout - - - Weight 2400 lbs. on hitch 300 lbs. - - - *Axle* —1½" drop, 10 leaf springs - - - *Hitch*—10,000 lb. with lifting device - - - Dead Air and Air Cell Insulation throughout trailer, roof and sides - - - Two roof ventilators, one in living quarters and one in vending compartment - - - 16" Counter inside 8" Counter outside. (Total Counter width 24" - - - Linoleum on floor and counters - - - Eleven light fixtures and air outlets - - - Special drop floor giving 36" work table only 48" height on outside, ground up - - - Partition separating living quarters from vending compartment, paneled door between - - - See price list for complete price details.

Aladdin Trailers for Commercial Use

The use of the automobile trailers in business is increasing at an astonishing pace. Its adaptation to the faster tempo of salesmanship is almost limitless. Trailers are being used by manufacturing and selling organizations to carry, DISPLAY AND SELL complete lines of samples—apparel—both men's and women's—glassware, silver, china, aluminum, cooking utensils, refrigerators, stoves, washing machines and all forms of household equipment, paints, hardware, auto accessories, shoes, sport goods, radios and musical instruments.

The list is too great to enumerate. Opportunity for display advertising on the body of the trailer provides a traveling signboard which is seen by from 20,000 to 50,000 people daily. Aladdin welcomes an opportunity to discuss this subject with business men.

Aladdin Trailer Adapted to Commercial Use in Covering State of Texas

Pitchmen, vaudeville troupes, circus people are going in for trailers.

—Fortune, 1937

ADAPTIVE USE OF TRAILERS. Many trailer manufacturers saw their product used in ways they couldn't imagine. Soon after, many companies began to offer trailers designed specifically for mobile showrooms, display units, and assorted food mobiles. Courtesy of Vintage Vacations.

ACSC MAP UNIT (facing) Panel truck-and-trailer combos exhibited in the courtyard of the Automobile Club of Southern California during World War II. Lower image shows an Airfloat trailer. Images courtesy of Auto Club of Southern California Archive.

QUARANTINE UNIT (above) California Coach exhibits their ready-to-go quarantine unit during World War II. Courtesy of USC Special Collections.

At first . . . the trailer was just something different in camping. Then people discovered you could live in them.

—*Fortune*, March 1937

WAR WORKERS' TRAILER CAMP (left), 1943. Stretching as far as the eye can see, trailers as temporary housing for war workers fill this site at one of the world's largest trailer camps near Portsmouth, Virginia. Twenty-three hundred trailers cover 290 acres. Courtesy of USC Special Collections.

AIRSTREAM TRAILER SURVIVES ATOMIC TEST (above) Virgil Sciullo, Treasurer, Ed Brown, Sales Manager and Art Costello, Vice President of Airstream Trailers, Inc., with the Airstream trailer that was to be used in an atomic-bomb test by the U.S. military. Radiation aside, this trailer survived very well, with only one broken window. Courtesy of USC Special Collections.

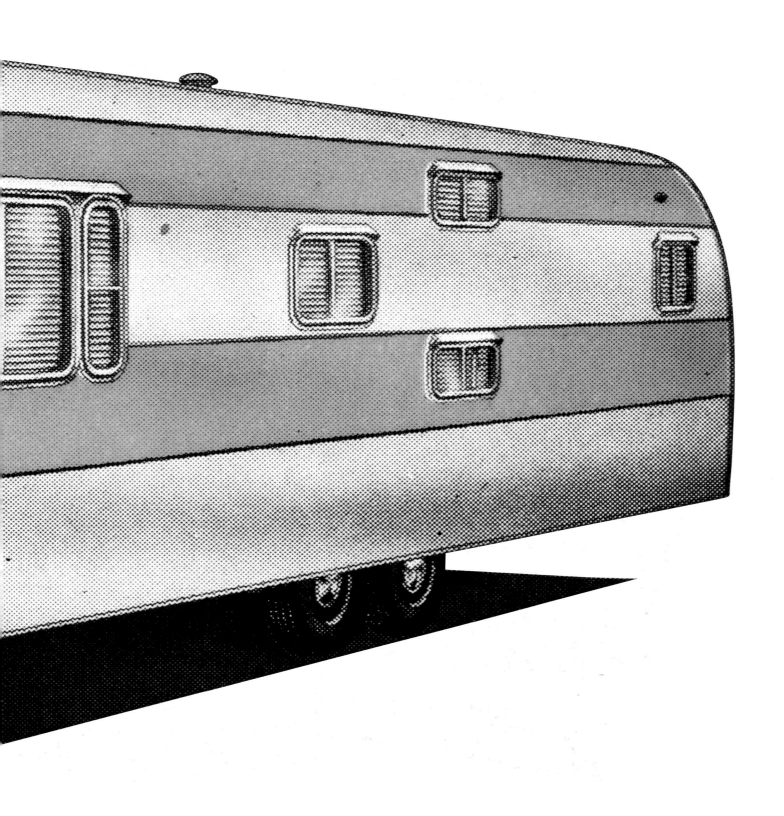

THE STAMINA TRAILER A name can make all the difference. Courtesy of Vintage Vacations.

According to most conservative trailer men, there will be a U.S. market of at least 400,000 units a year by 1940.

—*TIME*, 1921

TRAILER LOGOS

CREATING A MEMORABLE IMPRESSION

TRAVELEER LOGO (above) From the Traveleer company's letterhead. Courtesy of Vintage Vacations.
UNIVERSAL TRAILERS LOGO (left).

By the late thirties, over 400 companies were manufacturing trailers in the United States. None of the major auto makers like Ford, General Motors or Chrysler, had as yet entered the fray. Therefore, these new manufacturers were faced with the challenge not only of selling an unfamiliar brand but also an unknown commodity as trailers were still a relatively new thing. Price, style, size, and function were determining factors, of course, but trailer companies required an even bigger hook with which to reel in new customers.

What was needed then (and is still essential today) was legibility and good recognition value for the product. Companies would hopefully distinguish themselves with the trailers they built (Kozy Coach, Vagabond, and Roycraft were just a few that were ahead of the pack in the early days) but they were also compelled to set themselves apart from one another with catchy names and equally eye-catching logos.

The use of trademarks has existed for as long as there have been traders and merchants. Officially, they can be traced as far back as the thirteenth century and their function remains the same. What the successful logo states very simply is this: Here is our work and our craftsmanship, this is what we have to sell. And that's what trailer companies were attempting to do with bold and graphic logotypes. Some company names, like "Rollohome" or "Silver Streak," lent themselves to memorable word/image combinations while others, like the heart-sinking "Pacemaker," didn't. In the end, a well-designed logo couldn't guarantee a product's success but it could help things along.

Saratoga _TRAILER

PLATT
ELKHART INDIANA

WESTCRAFT
THE QUALITY LEADER

GLIDER TRAILER CO.

AVION

Rollohome
MARSHFIELD, WISCONSIN

TRAVEL TRAILERS

Glider Trailers

Travelo

KOZY
Coach

Landola

SPARTAN
The greatest Name in
TRAILERCOACHES

Star

Airstream

American

The VINDALE COACH Co.

Marlette Coach Co.

MARLETTE • MICHIGAN

the Lutes Coach

THE WORLD'S FINEST TRAILERS

NEW MOON

Fleetwood

Streamlite

Pacemaker

Richardson
TRAILER COACHES

Silver Streak TRAILER CO.

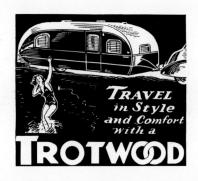
Travel in Style and Comfort with a **TROTWOOD**

PEERLESS

FLEETWHEELS COATES

United

STREAM-LITE TRAILER

Airfloat

ROYAL TRAILERS

ZIMMER TRAILER

Victor

Travelite
TRAILER COMPANY
of Texas

Stewart

KEN-CRAFT

Vagabond

LUXOR
Coach

Palace
Travel Coach

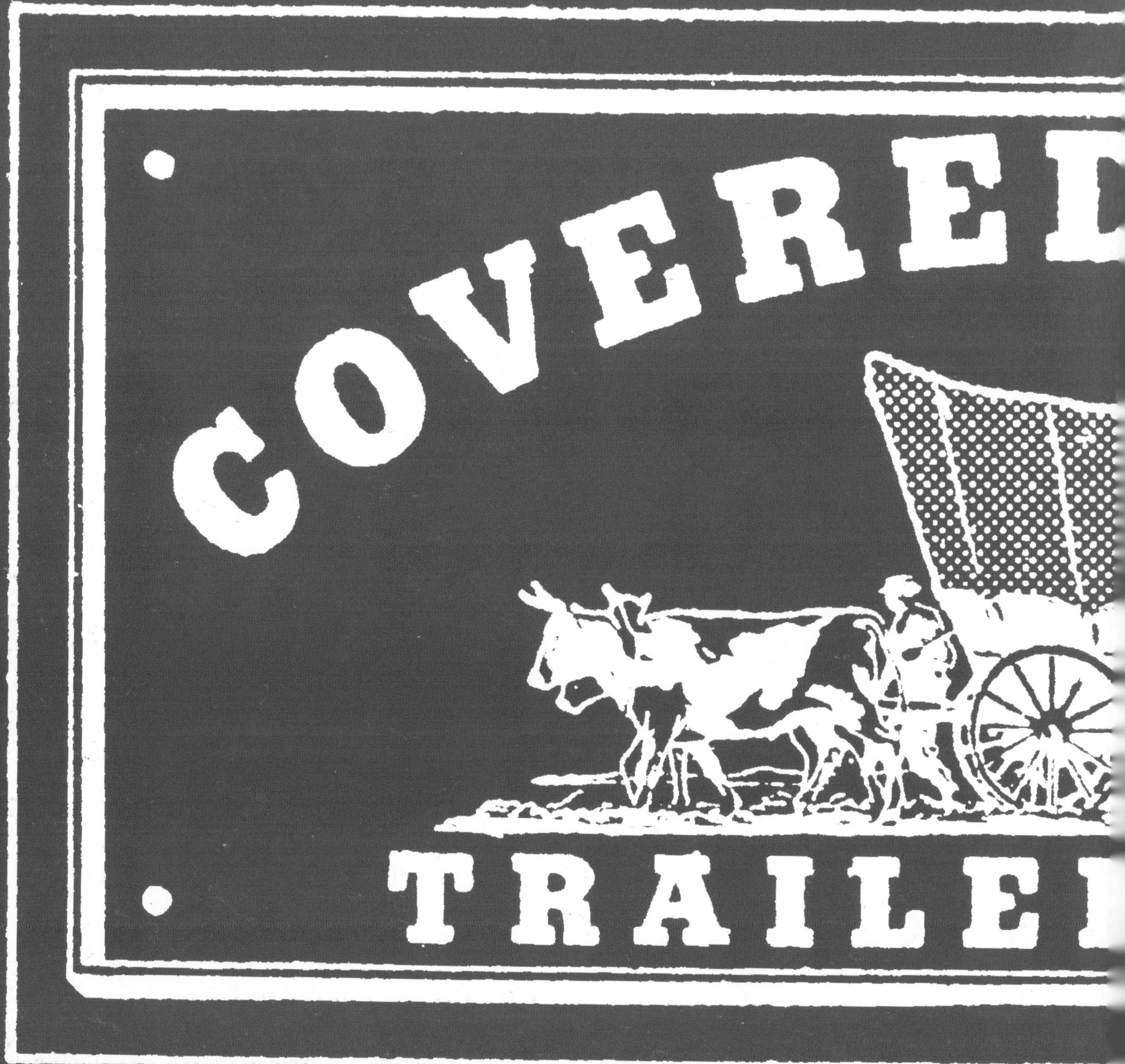
COVERED
TRAILE

WAGON HOMES

> Its shape was "a secret learned by listening to nature."
>
> —PAUL JARAY, ENGINEER, b.1889

TEARDROPS

KEEPING IT COMPACT

A favorite of do-it-yourself builders, the teardrop trailer emerged in the 1920s. Plans for the endearingly eccentric structures were published in magazines like *Popular Mechanics* and *Mechanix Illustrated.* Typically made from wood and masonite, teardrops had room for two to sleep comfortably and accommodated a cookstove under the rear hatch. The typical teardrop was, and still is, 4 feet wide, 4 feet high, and 8 to 10 feet long. As motor-camping grew in popularity, so, too, did the use of portable trailers like teardrops, and by the thirties, both teardrop kits and manufactured units became readily available. After World War II, teardrops, like most other trailers (and no small number of houses), were constructed from war-surplus aluminum and produced by companies such as Kustom Kamper, Kit Kamper, and King's Kamp Master (manufacturers who seem to have shared an inexplicably profound fear of the letter C).

But when America entered its peak years of postwar prosperity in the fifties, people were looking for more room for their newly acquired domestic gadgets from TVs to toasters. Even as trailerites were "getting away from it all," they wanted it all right there with them. So by the mid-sixties, as outsized recreational vehicles from companies like Winnebago and Fleetwood increased in popularity, tiny teardrops all but disappeared from the American landscape.

Yet these lovable underdogs were still around, tucked into backyards and garages across the country. At the tail end of the twentieth century, inspired by a growing trend in vintage trailer restorations, a few independent manufacturers with names as cute as the product they produced—like Tiny Tears and the Teardrop Fix-It Shop—emerged to take on the challenge of re-creating the teardrop trailer. Today, do-it-yourselfers continue to build their own and are some of the most passionate trailer owners you'll ever meet.

TEARDROP TRAILER (left) Courtesy of Auto Club of Southern California Archive.

TEARDROP SCHEMATIC DRAWING (above) Courtesy of the Teardrop Fix-It Shop.

JAN 1968

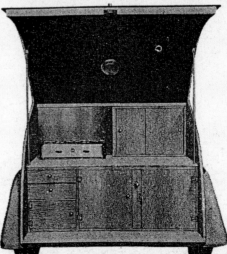

GENERAL TYPES OF TRAILERS

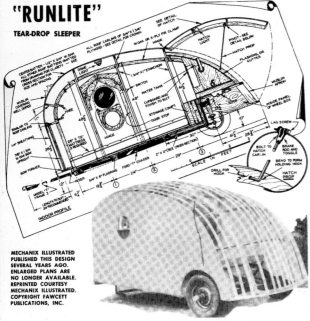

"RUNLITE"
TEAR-DROP SLEEPER

MECHANIX ILLUSTRATED
PUBLISHED THIS DESIGN
SEVERAL YEARS AGO.
ENLARGED PLANS ARE
NO LONGER AVAILABLE.
REPRINTED COURTESY
MECHANIX ILLUSTRATED.
COPYRIGHT FAWCETT
PUBLICATIONS, INC.

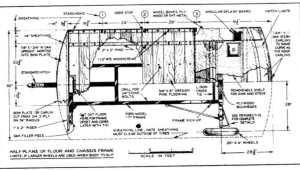

25

**TEARDROP ADVERTISEMENTS, PLANS AND
IMAGES** (above) Courtesy of Teardrop Fix-It Shop.

BUILD "WILD GOOSE"
A Sturdy Overnight Trailer

By Vic Goertzen

OVERNIGHT CAMPERS, hunters, fishermen and vacationers with limited time can appreciate the convenience, comfort and ready roadability of "Wild Goose." Hung low to the ground, yet with ample road clearance for the back trails, it tows anywhere your car will go. Keep it packed with the necessary bedding, also canned and dried foods and you can get away for a week-end trip in only a few minutes' time. When you arrive at the destination, Wild Goose sets up into a neat outdoor "kitchenette" in less time than it takes to put up a tent.

Looking over the details on the following pages you will note that the construction of this streamlined job differs somewhat from ordinary trailer construction. Where adaptations must be made only a few general dimensions have been given. Because the unit has been designed for road speeds up to 60 m.p.h. care must

be taken when assembling the welded chassis frame. When notching the channel-steel side frames to form the first bend, cut the notches accurately so the meeting edges fit snugly before welding. The gusset plates should be at least 12 in. long, and at the forward end of the drawbar where the reverse bends open the cuts made in the channel webs it's a good idea to weld in

Original Benroy Decal

11 Benroy Teardrops & 1 Benroy "Walkin" being loaded & shipped to Ft. Worth Tx. 1955

TEARDROP ADS, PHOTOGRAPHS AND PLANS
Courtesy of Teardrop Fix-It Shop.

All the comforts of home—complete to a telephone, that can be hooked to the main line—are incorporated in a trailer which Gloria Stuart, motion picture actress, had built especially for motion picture "sets" in the outdoors. The busy young man at the typewriter is Robert Kent, and the locale of this photo is in Mojave Desert.

Benroy

LENGTH, 10' Overall - WIDTH, 68" - WEIGHT, 760 lbs.

construction

- Varnished plywood interior
- All aluminum exterior
- Standard size tires (600x16)
- Two-inch angle frame
- Standard leaf spring undercarriage
- Two doors, each with opening windows
- Locking door handles
- Inside cabinets with shelves
- Three-quarter size mattress
- Standard 2-inch couplers

BENROY TRAILER PROD.

1024 WEST BURBANK BOULEVARD—BURBANK, CALIFORNIA

MODERNISTIC CAMPER

KEN-SKILL
Kustom Kamper

TEARDROP PHOTOGRAPHS (facing and above) The proud new owner of a teardrop. Courtesy of Delmar Watson.
KEN-SKILL LOGO (facing top) Courtesy of Teardrop Fix-It Shop.

OWD BILL JUNE JOHNNY DON
Brook Trout ETHEL

1952   Don - Bill - Bennett - Jack

Steelhead Trout - Klamath River

Brook trout Bennett Co. Don Bill Johnny Jack

Uncle Ernie - Salmon - Fern River Park

In the summer of 1951, my husband Jack, our two sons and myself went camping in northern California with a friend who had a teardrop trailer. All we had were some tents, a cookstove and all the essentials packed in boxes. We thought the teardrop trailer was such a great idea that before the summer of 1952 my husband built us one . . .

June Long

Benny—Ethel · Bill Bid June

June Rag Ethel

Get-together under Big Tree

He took a box utility trailer we had and built a top for it. He built cupboards inside for us to put our clothes and we put a mattress on the floor with our sleeping bags so we had our sleeping quarters. On the back when we raised the lid, he had built cupboards for our food, dishes and cooking utensils. He had also built a table where one end attached to the teardrop over the fender and the other end had some fold down legs and we had a nice work table. We used this set up for about 15 years . . .

OCT · 56

Parking lot at Coit Tower · Telegraph Hill · San Francisco

AUG · 56

Breaking up Camp getting ready to head for home

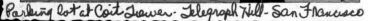

Big Tree

Ethel   June

Eating lunch · Ethel · Bennett · Mom Long

Every summer we went to Klamath California, to fish for Steelhead trout and salmon on the Klamath River. Only one year the fishing wasn't so good but the wild blackberries were great! So we picked wild blackberries and canned them and also made some jam. We canned 12 quarts of berries and 24 pints of jam per couple. When we were home we spent weekends at the Colorado River north of Yuma, Arizona. We traveled a lot with our teardrop and have a lot of good memories.

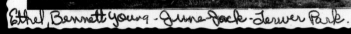

Ethel, Bennett Young - June Jock - Terwer Park.

Traveling along Hwy 395 in Mammoth Area.

Cajon Pass - Hwy 395

BIBLIOGRAPHY

Banham, Reyner. "Taking it With You," reprinted in *A Critic Writes: Essays by Reyner Banham.* Berkeley: University of California Press, 1996.

Boone, Andrew R. "Modern Gypsies." *Popular Science Monthly,* April 1937.

Brauer, Norman. *There to Breathe the Beauty: The Camping Trips of Henry Ford, Thomas Edison, Harvey Firestone, and John Burroughs.* Dalton, PA: Norman Brauer Publications, 1995.

Burkhart, Bryan, and David Hunt. *Airstream: The History of the Land Yacht.* San Francisco, CA: Chronicle Books, 2000.

Busch, Akiko. "Home on the Road." *Metropolis,* May 1995.

Byam, Wall. *Trailer Travel Here and Abroad: The New Way to Adventurous Living.* New York: David McKay Company, Inc., 1960.

Clifford, Harvey. "Back to the Covered Wagon." *Christian Science Monitor,* 7 October 1936.

Cooper, Morley. *The Trailer Book: How to Select, Equip, and Maintain a Modern Trailer Coach.* New York: Harper & Brothers, 1980.

Douglas, Lillie B. *Cape Town to Cairo.* Caldwell, ID: The Caxton Printers, Ltd., 1964.

Groene, Janet. *RVs: The Drive for Independence.* Louisville, KY: Crescent Hill Books, 1997.

"Hitting the Trail—1935 Style." *Popular Mechanics,* July 1935.

Jessup, Elon. *The Motor Camping Book.* New York: G.P. Putnam's Sons, 1921.

Jones, James. "Living in a Trailer." *Holiday,* August 1951.

Landau, Robert. *Airstream.* Layton, UT: Gibbs Smith, Publisher, 1984.

Leggett, Julian. "The Trailer Grows Up." *Popular Mechanics,* August 1939.

Long, J. C., and John D. Long. *Motor Camping.* Rahway, NJ: The Quinn & Boden Company, 1923, 1926.

McClelland, Thomas. "Motorhomes were envisioned 70 years ago by early motorists." *Slow Lane Journal,* May 1995.

Michaels, Mark. "America's Trailering Roots." *Trailer Life,* January 1998.

Nash, Charles Edgar. *Trailer Ahoy!* Lancaster, PA: Intelligencer Printing Company, 1937.

O'Brien, Howard Vincent. *Folding Bedouins or Adrift in a Trailer.* New York: Willett, Clark & Company, 1936.

Payne, Etta. *Home Was Never Like This: A Trailer's Eye View of Europe Today.* New York: Greenwich Book Publishers, 1957.

Pebworth, R.C. "Trailers Grow Up Into Houses Without Wheels." *Automobile and Trailer Travel,* June 1938.

Saunders, Lawrence. "Roll Your Own Home." *The Saturday Evening Post,* 23 May 1936.

Sibley, Hi. "Honeymoon House Trailer: Built With Dimes; Total Cost $60." *Mechanix Illustrated,* March-April 1939.

Smith, Jr., McGregor. *Thank You, Marco Polo: The Story of the First Around the World Trailer Caravan.* Coral Gables, FL: Wake-Brook House, 1966.

Smith, Philip H. "After Cars Come Trailers." *Scientific American,* February 1937.

Soderholm, Gertrude. "Housekeeping on Wheels—Killing Time in a Trailer." *Automobile and Trailer Travel,* February 1942.

Thornburg, David. *Galloping Bungalows: The Rise and Demise of the American House Trailer.* Hamden, CT: Archon Books, 1991.

"Trailerites Have Own Language . . . Here is Your Trailer Dictionary." The Trailer Coach Manufacturers Association's Official Trailer Coach Year Book, 1948.

Wallis, Allan D. *Wheel Estate: The Rise and Decline of Mobile Homes.* London: Oxford University Press, 1991.

White, Roger B. *Home on the Road: The Motor Home in America.* Washington, D.C.: The Smithsonian Institution Press, 2000.

Wilson, Alice. "You Can Take 'Em With You." *The Saturday Evening Post,* 14 August 1937.

"100 Years of RVing." *Trailer Life,* December 1999.

"200,000 Trailers." *Fortune,* March 1937.

For my very own trailerites: Lisa, Lily and Ryder

For Wally

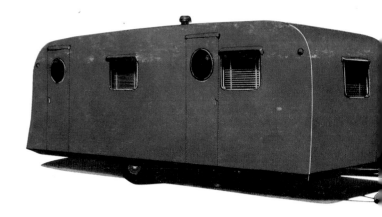